GW00648968

Marianne

MARIANNE VICELICH X

DRAMA
detox

Marianne

MARIANNE VICELICH X

Drama Detox
Published 2018

This hardback edition published in 2018.

British Library
Cataloguing-in-Publication entry
Author: Vicelich, Marianne
Title: Drama Detox/Vicelich, Marianne
ISBN: 978-0-9875518-8-7 (hbk.)

Design and layout—Jera Publishing
Printing—Haha Printing
First edition published in London, United Kingdom 2018
Orca Press

Orca Book Services Lt160 Milton Park
Abingdon Oxon
OX14 4SD
UNITED KINGDOM

DRAMA
detox

drama

(noun)

an exciting, emotional,
or unexpected event
or circumstance.

(noun)

a process or period of time in which one abstains from or rids the body of toxic or unhealthy substances; detoxification.

contents

"As we let our own light *shine,* we unconsciously give other people permission to do the same."

NELSON MANDELA

CHAPTER 1

Why are we attracted to drama?

WHAT IS DRAMA?

rama lives on the surface. The drama level of engagement is the "he said, she said, then this happened, and then she said, and then he said..." level. It is so easy to get caught up in it and start reacting to the emotions of a situation or story before pausing to consider how you want to respond.

For a lot of people, their lives are filled with a tonne of mini-dramas and fearful illusions. Yet often navigating drama is like trying to reverse the Titanic, with many of us left in the dark struggling to make sense of it all.

WHY DO WE ATTRACT DRAMA?

hy do you find yourself in dramatic scenarios? Boredom. Addiction to excitement. Restlessness. Letting the ego control our lives. Some people are attracted to drama like a moth to a flame. Chaos is a status quo for a lot of people. Many people say they hate drama, yet they keep attracting it. Maybe your close friend has as many catastrophes as there are days in the week. Maybe you are the person everyone calls with their problems. Or perhaps you unknowingly turn small issues into major crises and you would like to stop being so overwhelmed.

Whatever the case, you probably have at least a little drama in your life that you would like to minimise.

Drama is a form of self-sabotage that paradoxically we are drawn to. Your experiences with negativity and drama can be highly addictive patterns.

More often than not, we create our own drama during peaceful, calm stages in life. Why? When life is going too neutrally and too equilibriously, people have a tendency to get bored and discontented really easily. It's almost as if we strive for peace and happiness, yet when we're living it, it's not enough.

If you were told that your life could either be a slow, steady and persistent train ride, or an adrenaline, pulsing, blood-screaming roller-coaster, which would you choose? Many people seem to be under the impression that to live life to the fullest is to recklessly seek out situations that they believe will add meaning, significance, and fulfillment to their lives.

It feels terrible to be around people that cause drama. They leave you feeling exhausted and not feeling terribly good about yourself.

How often have you sabotaged your own happiness by creating your own drama? If there is drama in multiple areas of your life then undeniably you are the constant. We don't do anything repeatedly unless there's something in it for us, so what's the payoff?

WHO ARE THESE PEOPLE
THAT CAUSE DRAMA?

hosen friends, partners, employees and acquaintances. Or unchosen family, neighbours and work colleagues.

DRAMA GETS ATTENTION

ince drama uses the same mechanisms in the brain as opiates people can become easily addicted to drama. It causes the pituitary gland and hypothalamus to secrete endorphins which are pain-suppressing and pleasure-inducing compounds which opiates mimic. Thereby drama eases the anxiety of wanting more attention than you are getting. Like any addiction, you build up a tolerance that continuously requires more to get the same neurochemical effect. This means that you need more and more drama to get the same thrill.

detox

WHY WE ARE PROGRAMMED
FOR DRAMA?

*I*t all stems back to our childhood. As a child you learn specific beliefs about love, happiness, peace, drama from your family. For example, you might have grown up seeing and believing that love comes with lots of yelling and lots of conflict (drama). As a result, this is your normal. Your comfort zone is the equivalent to a lot of discomfort. So when you experience comforting love, peace, and kindness this might inspire anxiety because it's not familiar. As a result you might choose scenarios which are familiar to you and that's how you wind up surrounded by drama constantly. Your subconscious has a goal to find a relationship which matches up with the pain that you find familiar from childhood. You will allow pain and drama into your life. You might also self-sabotage your happiness to bring yourself to that comfort level that you are familiar with.

The repetition of our past into the present is know as repetition compulsion. Freud believed we have two ways of keeping the past alive in our present. We can do it through our thoughts or our actions. Your familiar past can encroach into your present by encouraging those thoughts and actions. On the flip side if you grew up in a loving family you will not allow pain and suffering (drama) into your friendships and life. You will repel this behaviour and you will not seek out drama.

You must accept that a lot of the negative patterns in your present come from limiting beliefs developed in your past stemming from negative childhood rein-forcement. Self love and positive belief patterns will help you disengage from past negativity. Get clear about the fact that this negativity from your past has interfered with your life and has created the drama into present.

CHAPTER 2

How to drama detox your life

AIM TO FIND ALTERNATIVE SOLUTIONS

*I*f you are looking for attention, can you get it more directly? If you are bored, what new adventure can you create to your life?

The first important step in 'detoxing drama' from your life is to recognise and acknowledge it.

BECOME AWARE OF A 'DRAMA IN THE MAKING'

*A*wareness enables you to detach from pre-programmed thoughts and emotions so you can observe your actions. You then realise that your thoughts, and the emotions they produce are dysfunctional and unnecessary. Once you can observe your actions, in the present moment as they occur, you are able to respond from a rational mind, rather than react from false, elevated emotions.

Find a person who is honest, and cares enough about you to tell you the truth, even when you don't want to hear it. Use creative outlets to lessen your baseline stress levels such as meditation or yoga. Act as if you are not a drama addict and a compulsive attention seeker and the more you do that the more efficiently those neurons will fire.

CHANGE YOUR PERSPECTIVE

A lot of drama takes place in our heads, and it's usually because we are too deeply immersed in a difficult situation to recognise it isn't as dire as it seems.

If you see yourself getting overwhelmed by a situation, step back and realise this feeling isn't permanent — nothing is. Then focus on action steps — on the things that you can control.

DON'T FEED INTO OTHER PEOPLE'S DRAMA

If someone repeatedly comes to you with catastrophes, give yourself a window of time when you will listen, then take care of your own needs by walking away. Take an inventory of which people in your life leave you feeling stressed and unhappy more often than not. If you don't want to completely remove a toxic relationship, minimise the time you spend together. If you don't want to change how often you see each other, recognise the drama triggers.

Essentially, you get what you put out. If you act in a way that is positive with minimal drama, you attract the same kind of positive situations and people.

A lot of drama comes from poor communication and confusion. Eliminate it by finding the courage to say exactly what you mean. It may be harder in the moment, but it can save a lot of heartache in the long run.

Sometimes what we are labelling as drama is just someone who really needs us. Instead of expelling mental energy judging the situation as good or bad, focus on being there and being a friend in the moment.

LEARN FROM DRAMA

Sometimes it seems like drama happens to us, and we are powerless to remove ourselves from the cause. Another perspective is that every time we find ourselves immersed in something that seems overwhelming, we have an opportunity to learn how to deal with challenges better.

Life will always involve mini fires that we feel desperate to put out. If we can learn to fan them, they may actually be able to light our way in a more constructive and positive way forward.

13

CHAPTER 3

Is drama bad for us?

WHAT DOES DRAMA DO TO YOU?

- It causes you to be stressed out and tired
- Creates overwhelm and sensitivity
- Perpetuates a feeling of lack and unworthiness
- Leaves you forgetful with a lack of focus
- Makes your relationships difficult
- Allows you to experience burn out and constant negativity

Drama has the power to influence your emotional and physical nature. It can cause:

- Loss or gain in appetite
- Problems with sleep
- Anxiety and stress
- Depression

Stress can also physically damage your heart muscle. Drama that brings forth stress damages your heart because stress hormones increase your heart rate and constrict your blood vessels. This forces your heart to work harder and increases your blood pressure. According to the American Institute of Stress, the incidence rate of heart attacks and sudden death increases after major stress-inducing incidents. When dramatic episodes are life changing and can cause an individual to feel like the world is against them.

Outlets such as nutritional health are one of the most widely effected elements associated with drama. Some people don't eat while others binge eat to numb the drama. These traits live inside of us and tend to come out when drama arises. Researchers at the University of Miami found that when people are placed in stressful situations, they are likely to consume 40 per cent more food then normal.

Drama is inevitable. However, unnecessary drama can be avoided. Distance yourself from people that bring constant drama into your life. Take action within your own life events to avoid dramatic situations — you are your biggest preventative.

Recognise when you may be engaging in a dramatic way:

- Are you trying to receive sympathy or other forms of attention from others all the time?

- Focusing on someone else's issues instead of your own

- Giving yourself a great excuse to procrastinate

- Feeling needed, either by rescuing others or by being rescued

detox

RECOGNISE WHEN YOU MIGHT
BE CREATING DRAMA

*Y*ou get what you put out. If you act in a way that is positive and minimal drama, you attract the same kind of positive situations and people. When you minimise drama with your-self, you magnetise that energy, so the world around you seems focused and calm.

Are you looking for attention or excitement? Did you grow up with drama and you just feel at ease when there is some around you?

When we look beyond the drama, we are able to see what is going on much clearly. What really happened or is happening.

NOW AIM TO FIND
ALTERNATIVE SOLUTIONS

A lot of the drama takes place in our own heads, and it is usually because we are too deeply immersed in a difficult situation to recognise that it isn't as bad as it seems.

You need to ask yourself, "What is my role in perpetuating this situation? What is my role in what is happening now? How do I choose to engage going forward?"

If you are overwhelmed by a given situation, step back from it. Then focus on the action steps — the things you can control.

- Build a reputation as not participating in drama. Resist the urge to participate. Often people calm themselves down when other people don't validate their drama.

- Minimise dramatic people in your life. Befriend only people with good energy that don't promote or create drama.

detox

- ⁘ Recognise drama triggers. When the conversation moves towards drama, change it.
- ⁘ Be clear and straight with people.
- ⁘ Be open and honest when you communicate with people.

If you have an issue with someone, don't talk to other people about it as gossip breeds drama. Drama evolves due to a misunderstanding, confusion or an overaction. Eliminate it by finding the courage to say exactly what you mean. Also, let people know they can be honest with you. If someone thinks they need to walk on eggshells around you, they will likely hold things in, it will eventually come out. This can manifest itself in resentful actions or words.

IT IS NOT ALWAYS DRAMA

Sometimes what we are labelling as drama is just someone who really needs us. When it comes to people that you love, always take an extra moment to reconsider, if the "problem" is actually a problem. Focus on being there and being a friend in the moment. Don't take on people's negative energy, just focus on being present and constructive.

Sometimes it seems like drama happens to us, and we are powerless to remove ourselves from the cause. Another perspective is that every time we find ourselves immersed in something that seems overwhelming, we have an opportunity to learn how to deal with challenges better.

WHAT IS YOUR DEFAULT LEVEL?

ver the next few days, pay close attention to how you respond to situations and circumstances in your life — to challenges. conflicts, and opportunities. Try to look for solutions rather than impulsive reactions.

CHAPTER 4

Why do people love drama?

Drama does not
    just walk into
your life.
    Either you create it,
    invite it, or
associate with it.

REALITY #1

People can live very boring lives.

REALITY #2

People are desperate for some excitement.

REALITY #3

People can be boring.

REALITY #4

Drama can give them the edge
and excitement they crave.

EXCESSIVE ATTENTION SEEKING
AND DRAMA ADDICTION

*E*xcessive attention seeking is not a character flaw. It is a brain wiring response to early developmental trauma caused by neglect. The developing brain observes its environment and wires itself accordingly to survive in that world that it presumes will be like those experiences. Newborns are extremely dependent on getting their Mother's attention for survival. The more their needs are neglected during early development the more the child equates getting attention with survival and safety. In turn, the more he or she develops the belief system that it is necessary to go to whatever lengths to get attention. When a child is not able to get attention from his or her primary caretakers, he or she will do what kids do and act out by saying or doing something that creates drama. Children do this as negative attention is still attention. We expect this because children are trying to work out boundaries.

Drama gets attention. Drama causes the pituitary gland and hypothalamus to secrete endorphins, which are the pain-supressing and pleasure-inducing compounds, which heroin and other opiates mimic. Therefore, drama eases the anxiety of wanting more attention than you are getting. Naturally, since drama uses the same mechanisms in the brain as opiates, people can easily become addicted to drama. Like any addiction, you build up a tolerance that continuously requires more to get the same neurochemical affect. In the case of drama, it means that you need more and more to get the same thrill.

Creating this kind of drama in an adult relationship is at best a sad commentary on an obvious broken communication dynamic. In addition, it wastes the most precious thing you have, your time. Attention-seeking behaviour is just plain exhausting for everyone involved.

A little drama here and there is a part of life, but making it a lifestyle will not allow you to find peace. If you are invested in being a drama queen, you need to take a look at why you think this behaviour is okay.

Ask yourself why do you need all the attention? There may be some insecurity or self-esteem issues going on for you.

detox

If you tolerate attention-seeking behaviour, you need to start setting some strong boundaries. If you tolerate bad behaviour, you will simply encourage it to continue happening. Being with someone who continually makes you feel wrong, guilty, or not good enough is not going to make you happy. Find a way to delve deep to fix it.

ATTENTION-SEEKING AS AN ARTICULATION OF PAIN

*A*ttention-seeking behaviour comes about as a response to deeply painful trauma or psychological disturbance and it reflects a desperate attempt to cope with overwhelming emotional turmoil. Rather than minimising, trivialising, or ascribing malicious intent to these acts, it is vital that we search for meaning and understanding to help someone who is crying out in pain.

A dramatic person is someone who reacts to everyday events with excessive emotion and behaves in theatrical, attention-grabbing ways. They worship you one minute and despise you the next, based on overreactions to minor events.

Living or working with someone like that can be draining and disturbing. Such a colleague can curtail your productivity at the office or even shut down teams as everyone tries to contain the chaos. If you live with drama, you may be bombarded daily with accusations, leaving you feeling angry, guilty and exhausted.

HOW TO DIFFUSE DRAMA?

When we are safely on the sidelines, drama can be funny or fascinating. We have no problem with hyperbole and hysteria as long as we are not directly effected by it. But plant these tribulations in our own lives, and it's not nearly as much fun. Sure, dramatic people may reel us in with their charisma and vulnerability — but the charm comes with a price. That's because they violate the primary rule of a good relationship. A balance of give and take, nourished by mutual listening, empathy, interest, and respect. Dramatic people crave admiration and attention, but can't and won't give it back.

When we work with one days often consist of putting out their fires. If we live with one, exhaustion, recrimination and threat negotiation are daily occurrences.

The result is that we are sucked dry. with less time, energy, and enthusiasm to fuel our own lives. And that's a shame, because we are putting ourselves second to other people's demands.

EMOTIONAL VAMPIRES

*D*rama can wreck havoc in your life if you don't guard yourself. If a person you are connected to shows signs of three or more of these behaviours, it might be a good idea to rethink your relationship.

HYPERBOLE

Every molehill is a mountain.

WHAT THEY DO?

- Spin small anxieties into a disaster.
- Cry wolf at the slightest sign of trouble.
- Obsess over unattainable ideals of beauty and wealth.
- Over exaggerate stories or people they know.

WHAT DOES IT DO TO YOU?

You lose your sense of perspective, either adopting a sceptical outlook or assuming a disaster is around every corner.

ACCUSATION

Dramatic people are quick to point fingers
rather than take responsibility.

WHAT THEY DO?

- Throw others under the bus.
- Find a scrapegoat every time
  they screw up.
- Take minor provocations as
  personal affronts.

WHAT IT DOES TO YOU?

You walk on eggshells around them. You feel guilty
when good things happen to you.

LIMELIGHTING

When the spotlight slips from their
self-serving interpretation of the world,
they find ways to steal it back.

WHAT THEY DO?

- Display volatile mood shifts.
- Cry hysterically or make other theatrical shows of vulnerability.
- Talk all about them, them, them and expect you to listen to the monologue.
- Never remember what's going on with you.
- Dominate social gatherings with personal stories and demands.
- Over-share, regardless of what is socially appropriate.
- Betray secrets.
- Make threats.

WHAT DOES IT DO TO YOU?

Your self-esteem is effected as you are left in the wings.

detox

HOW TO OVERCOME DRAMA?

*P*sychiatrists say that drama behaviour is wired into the brain, due to a varying combo of genetics, trauma and other environmental factors.

If this person is not willing to change, it is best to focus on changing your behaviour so that you can keep your positive energy in check. Follow these six steps to keep yourself from being drained by a person who asks a lot without contributing positively to your life.

STEP 1

CONFRONT YOUR OWN
FASCINATION WITH DRAMA.

The common denominator is you. Ask yourself: Does a dramatic person's neediness make you feel important? Do you feel a sense of superiority over such people? Taking stock of your own contribution can help you shift away from them.

STEP 2

DECODE THEIR LANGUAGE.

You rush to the aid of a dramatic friend again and again, only to find there is nothing wrong. When you interpret what they are really saying, you are less likely to go over the edge with them.

STEP 3

SET BOUNDARIES.

Create some strong personal boundaries and don't allow them to step over you. Be firm and strict with your time and energy.

STEP 4

DON'T REWARD THEIR BEHAVIOUR

When they behave out of line, do not give them more attention. If they insult you, threaten, are demanding and cause drama, don't respond to them. Take a deep breath, practice gratitude and stay calm.

DECODING DRAMA LANGUAGE

WHAT THEY ARE SAYING	WHAT THEY ARE DOING	WHAT ITS ACTUALLY MEANS
Don't tell anyone but....	GAINING ATTENTION	Nothing is sacred. They can't keep a secret. They will risk anything for attention.
You never believed in me...	DEFLECTING BLAME	They blame others for everything. They don't accept responsibility
Everyone hates me....	EXAGGERATING	They are spinning into negativity because they didn't get the attention they wanted.

STEP 5

REPLENISH YOURSELF

To recharge after an encounter with drama, go for a walk or meditate or play music. Don't dwell on the drama because it will only keep you in the negative zone.

STEP 6

WHEN ALL ELSE FAILS, DISTANCE YOURSELF.

If you have tried steps 1–5 and you are still feeling frazzled, you might have to cut ties. Tell them you need time alone to focus on yourself. Likely, their antics won't end, so stop answering their calls. Yes they will make you feel guilty, but ultimately, if you want things to change, be the one to implement this change.

CHAPTER 5

35 day drama detox affirmations

detox

People who are not
happy with their lives
will often try to start
drama in yours.

As we become older, we become more honest and don't have the patience for pointless drama.

detox

Sometimes it's better to
react with no reaction.

Being strong doesn't
always mean you
have to fight the battle.
True strength is being
mature to walk away
from the nonesense with
your head held high.

45

detox

If you bring nothing but drama to the table, don't be surprised if everyone else gets up and leaves.

I refuse to entertain negativity. Life is too big and time is too short to get caught up in empty drama.

detox

Walk away from anything
that gives you bad vibes.
There is no need to explain
or make sense of it. It's
your life. So do what
makes you happy.

A lot of the happiness or unhappiness in your life is a result of the people you're surrounding yourself with so develop the courage to let go of those toxic people.

detox

Don't let someone who
doesn't like themselves
make you hate yourself.

Maturity starts

when drama ends.

detox

Live a life without drama.

I love straight forward people. The lack of drama makes life so much easier.

detox

A life filled with drama indicates that a person is disconnected from purpose and meaningful goals. People with purpose don't have time for drama.

Life becomes so much better when you decide not to care. Just live for the moment and don't let the drama bring you down.

detox

Beautiful things happen
in your life when you
distance yourself from all
the negativity and drama.

Never let somebody's drama determine the outcome of your day.

detox

There is a time in life when
you have to let go of all
the pointless drama and
the people who create it.

The amount of times that
you say you hate drama
is directly proportional
to the amount of times
you actually create it.

detox

Negative people need
drama like oxygen.

Some people create their own storms, then get upset when it rains.

detox

A real woman avoids
drama, she knows her time
is precious and she's not
wasting it on unimportant
people or things.

Anything that costs you

your peace is too expensive.

detox

Sometimes you have to let
people go because they
are toxic to you. Let them
go because they take and
take and leave you empty.

Let them go because in
the ocean of life when all
you're trying to do is stay
afloat, they are the anchor
that's drowning you.

detox

Don't allow silly drama
to stress you out.
Breathe and let it go.

If you are tired of
drama in your life, just
quit being the actor.

detox

Remember you were
happy before they came
into your life and you
can be just as happy
again when they leave.

People with purpose,
goals and visions have
no time for drama. They
invest their energy in
creativity and focus on
living a positive life.

detox

The best apology is
changed behaviour.

Sometimes you just have to erase the messages, delete the numbers and move on. You don't have to forget who that person was to you; only accept that they aren't that person anymore.

Drama is hate. Drama is pushing your pain onto others. Drama is destruction. Some take pleasure in creating drama while others make excuses to stay stuck in drama. I choose not to step into a web of drama that I can't get out of.

MARIANNE VICELICH

Don't react to toxic
people. Not giving them
a reaction when they
desperately seek it, is
far more powerful.

detox

If there seems to be drama
wherever you go, consider
the fact that you might
be the one bringing it.

I honestly love being around positive people. You are not judged, there's no drama, everyone just wants to relax and have a nice time.

detox

Never be afraid of change.
You may lose something
good, but you may gain
something even better.

Turn up the music and
turn down the drama.

CHAPTER 6

Practice self-care

ne of the steps to eliminating drama from your life is adopting self-love as a daily practice. Self-love is how you are meant to feel about yourself. It is the key to being you. It's how you honour yourself. It reveals your secret beauty. It shows your true value. As you commit to loving yourself more, you understand yourself better, you get what being true to yourself means, and you learn how to enjoy being you. It is the hidden ground that helps you to meet every challenge with a big heart. It empowers you to take your place in your life and to show the world what you are really made of.

Self nurturing is the focus point in creating a new present and positive future. We repeat what we don't heal and repair. Drama will follow you wherever you go unless you release it. The time has come to repair your anger and resentment about the past so that you can live a happier present.

When you love yourself enough, you quit settling for too little and you began to see that you don't have to chase after life. If you are quiet and hold still, life comes to you. Quit exhausting yourself by trying so hard, and you will began to feel a community within. This inner team with diverse talents and idiosyncrasies will be your strength and inner guidance. I became my own authority by listening to the wisdom of my heart.

- Take a deep breath.
- Think of three things to be thankful for.
- Let the gratitude flow through you ... smile.
- Passion takes you places ... .
- Accomplishment makes us happy. Never underestimate the power that lies in work.
- Build confidence by completing tasks you set out to do.

detox

Treat yourself with dignity and appreciation.

Be assured that you are a highly capable individual.

Let go.

Express gratitude for all that you have been blessed with.

Take proactive action that is beneficial for you every day.

Get off your anger/fear treadmill. Nourish your inner strength and enhance the over-all quality of your life by reducing anger and fear related stress.

Define daily personal goals and sustain the effort to achieve them.

Use positive self-talk to re-frame your mood in a positive light.

Expand your vision. Think of five things that are interesting to you, then make the decision to start engaging in them.

Lead a full life. Have lots to do. Meet people. Engage in interesting and fun activities. Love your work. Mastering the art of being busy and independently active is the key. Poet Gregory Corso wrote that standing on a street corner waiting for no-one is power, and it is absolutely without question the truth.

Resistance is so draining. There is a beauty to gracious acceptance, an energy that leads to peace. In a vexing situation try laughing rather than snarling, try combating with a light heart. You will ultimately be the winner — for you will have the gift of serenity. Try letting go of the situation you cannot control, the one that's sapping your energy and churning your sleep. Flood your life with the relief of walking away, with dignity.

Live with confidence and joy. There is so much wonder and beauty in this world. Seek it.

Quit fearing your fear. Quit rehashing the past and worrying about the future. Keep in the present where aliveness lives. Realise that your mind can torment and deceive you, but in the service of your heart, it is a great and noble ally.

detox

Try not to get caught in the abyss of emotions, because emotions ebb and flow. You can't hold onto a raft of sadness always, eventually that emotion will go out to sea and you won't always be sad. Pessimists take things personally, and believe that their situation is permanent and that problems are pervasive. Optimists are the opposite as they understand that things change. They believe that their situation is transient and it will pass. Both happiness and sadness are not lasting.

Use your anger for something positive and good. Don't let a situation be complicated by your negativity.

Don't be afraid of sharing your vulnerabilities — your fear, envy, frustration. It will make you realise that you are not alone as your vulnerabilities are shared by many.

THE TRANSFORMATIVE EFFECT
OF KEEPING A JOURNAL ...

*W*riting in a journal is a great way to release energy and patch the soul when it is wounded. It is a great creative resource as well. What you write — be it the details of your personal life, concepts or snippets and stories from your day — is up to you. A journal can be a great way to let off some steam or deal with pent-up energies.

A journal is a particularly effective means to delve into feelings. It is a place to have a one-way conversation about anything you like. You can express feelings, ideas or fears there without ever having to worry about what someone will say. For the time you are writing in the journal, it is all about what you are feeling in a secure and safe environment.

KINDNESS ...

*K*indness is an indispensable virtue from which most of the other virtues flow, the wellspring of our happiness. It assumes and does not demand that others will reciprocate and is in that way determinedly optimistic. Kindness shelters a variety of highly valued traits — empathy, generosity, unselfishness, tolerance, acceptance, and compassion.

COURAGE ...

*T*he essence of courage is overcoming fear. The ability to sustain the inevitable disappointments that life deals each of us and respond with a determination not to be defeated is one of the highest forms of courage.

HELPING OTHERS

*A*lmost every study of longevity indicates one secret that makes people healthier and happier and that's helping others. Some research shows a 60 per cent decrease in mortality figures among those who help others. They are aided by what's called the 'helpers' high. Specifically, it is the dignity, the joy, the passion, and the purpose of helping others. Research shows that people who donate money are happier than people with the same amount of money who don't donate at all.

Helping others inspires gratitude for what life has given you, and this is what really turbocharges your happiness, and helps you define your purpose in life.

FINDING AUTHENTICITY

*M*ost of our lives are spent driven by external factors and motivators (striving for that pay rise or promotion) as opposed to intrinsic ones with a higher ideal (a love of the work you do or a purpose). So to find our true, authentic self and to be happy with what we find, we must know how we exist in relationship to other things — specifically to other people and to the world at large. When we break through the instincts and the habits, we break through a level of superficiality that many people typically tend to live with. And that's when we break through to a deeper experience in life.

STAY SIMPLE

appiness is really rooted in simplicity. Excessive thoughts and actions diminish it. Excesses cloud basic values. One reason is that motivation is about removing extraneous stimuli so you can focus emotionally on the important task at hand. In the end, happiness comes from filling ones heart with love while practicing charity and dispensing kindness.

Above all else, love makes everything right. When you come back to the love you have in your heart for your friends, and family and for your own life, you feel at peace.

Go where you are wanted and stray from where you aren't. Surround yourself with positive people and environments. Don't waste your time with people who don't appreciate and value you for everything you have to offer. One of the keys to lasting relationships and friendships is mutual respect. Don't squander your time chasing anyone who has told you they don't want you around. Evaluate all your relationships and weed out the negative ones.

Each of us has a purpose on this beautiful earth. What we make of our lives and how we choose to fulfill it is up to us. What is most important is that you have a cause, something you believe in that lights up your life and connects you with your life's purpose.

Find something in life that makes you get up in the morning, and keep on doing that. Stand up for things you believe in.

I am a firm believer that everything happens for a reason. I don't believe in coincidences, I think that things happen the way they are supposed to. When you really look at and evaluate every experience you have had, it's a direct result of your actions and thoughts. Don't fight or wish away unexpected occurrences. In time, and in its own way, it proves to better your life in some way.

As we come into our own life and begin to climb up our personal ladders of success, we must be cautious to leave our egos behind and not allow them to interfere with the integrity and honesty of our work. Your ego will always be close behind, chasing you, nipping at your heels as you move up in this world. So don't let it get ahead of you.

YOUR SURROUNDINGS

*P*eople will come in and out of your life. Not everyone's going to know how to make you feel good, but don't get hung up on that — just let it go. The people who stay are the ones who make you feel wonderful. The next time someone says something that hurts you, visualise it as a bead of water that rolls right off you.

Things come to you for the right reasons at the right time so don't resist them. Surrender to these gifts and challenges with grace and ease. Wherever you are fighting today, surrender to it.

detox

YOUR HIGHEST LEVEL

*I*n order to bring the highest version of yourself to everything you do, you must be performing at your highest level. That means making sure you get enough sleep, eat well, exercise, meditate, and take care of your mind, body and soul. Sometimes we think we have to show how hard we work by burning ourselves out, but I promise you it's so much better to find the balance. You will feel happier, you will be more productive, and your work will be better.

EXPECTATIONS

*E*xpectations are just disappointments waiting to happen. When we spend our time waiting for things to happen we are not living in the now and we set ourselves up to be let down and end up judging ourselves, which only makes us feel worse. It's important to know what you want for your life. At the same time it's also important to be open to how and where those dreams will be fulfilled. The problematic thing about expectations is that it builds our hopes up too high. It's wonderful to be a dreamer but it's also important to be grounded and realistic.

Release your expectations, stay open to the journey, and explore what is right in front of you.

IN THE END

Love is the ultimate healer, the best remedy. Loves makes all things possible. It empowers us and allows us to become more open and compassionate than we ever dreamed, there is no such thing as loving too much. People will be grateful that you are able to love with all your heart. Use your love and the love from others to heal yourself.

detox

DON'T SAVE IT FOR LATER

If you are constantly waiting for the perfect time,
You'll usually miss the right time.
Lean towards the spontaneous side:
Trust your intuition, go with the flow.
Use your wisdom, learnt from the past,
But the future is already starting.

SELF ESTEEM ...

The concept of self-esteem dovetails into multiple facets of you. It is connected to your sense of worth and feelings of efficacy, and it pertains to a personal evaluation of yourself. In an ideal world, you would hold a very high opinion of yourself, which you would use to establish your core or set point — the rules or schemas you use to navigate your life. Unfortunately, this is not always the case, as you may look externally for validation or to gain perspective on where you stand in life, relying on these external opinions and views as a measure of your own self-worth.

While most of us would assert that we were raised to believe that our inner worth is inviolate and intrinsic, when life pitches us a curveball, doubts can mess up our game and shake our resolve.

Criticism is merely a report from another person that points out disapproval with respect to some action, opinion, or behaviour, in other words, it shouldn't be a frightening prospect. One of the seminal features of cognitive behaviour therapy is the stubborn refusal to buy in to an individual's sense of worthlessness. Take a look at what your internal editor says when you face criticism and pressure from others to conform, or even worse when you berate yourself. Develop a new script.

If you still insist you are not worthy make a list of your supposed worthiness to try to prove it to yourself. Do the maths. In short you will discover that the so-called hard evidence you present to yourself to back up your "worthless theory" will be nonsense.

Fight the negative messages you are so often exposed to and build up your self-esteem.

Learn from criticism. If you feel that what you are hearing is constructive, heed it. If you think it is cruel disregard it.

Release, relax, and remember these words can only hurt you if you let them. Your self-worth does not depend upon someone else's opinion of you.

Self-worth cannot solely be built through what you do. Of course achievements can bring you satisfaction, but they are not autonomously responsible for true happiness.

These affirmations will help to empower you even in difficult times....

- I respect myself for who I am, not merely for what I do

- I have skills and attributes, talents and passions

- I have ambitions, I know that I can achieve what I set out to do

- I am kind and honest, and I believe in the good in life

- I appreciate my body and feel happy to be alive. I treat myself well, and I pray for strength and compassion

- I am worthy, valid and a worthwhile individual

CHAPTER 7

Live a life of purpose

THE PURPOSE OF LIFE IS
A LIFE OF PURPOSE

*I*f we follow our intuition, we will find our purpose. We all have gifts and our purpose is related to these. Consider if you are living a fulfilling life with purpose. If the answer is 'no', then it's important to understand the influence of your thoughts and beliefs on your sense of purpose. Remember that our positive and negative traits can be like two sides of a coin. A strength, such as being determined, can also be viewed as a negative quality at times — determination may be viewed as stubbornness. Sometimes we only view the negative aspect. We might need to work on enhancing our sense of self-belief. Remember to celebrate our successes and achievements. Sometimes you just need to have faith that things will work out, that sometimes we need to take a leap of faith, trusting that we know ourselves and will end up where we need to go. Keep your focus on that which gives us energy, for which we have passion, and to move with trust in that direction.

TAP INTO POSITIVITY

ositive emotions make us more receptive and more creative, opening us up to possibilities and intuitive experiences.

Practice loving-kindness towards yourself and others.

Compassion involves letting go of judgements, when we do this we are more able to be intuitive and our heart grows.

Practicing acts of kindness can help bring more peace and joy to our life.

If we follow our intuition and passion, we will find our purpose.

Purpose is about doing what we love and were meant to do.

HAPPINESS IS . . .

AN ATTITUDE

The most wasted day is that in which we have not laughed ...

Happiness happens inside-out, not outside-in. There is no magical formula that states that X per cent of status or wealth will guarantee happiness. To be happy, you must think yourself happy. Happiness is the product of mind, of attitude and of thought. Happiness comes from you, not to you.

A PERCEPTION

If you look for happiness, happiness will find you. Many people make themselves unhappy in life because they look for all the things in life they either haven't got or cannot have, they rarely take the time to look at, acknowledge and appreciate all that they have got.

A TALENT

Happiness is not a gift given to the chosen few. Happiness is a talent and a skill. Happiness is like a muscle — it needs to be flexed and exercised. Happiness happens if you let it and is only ever a thought or feeling anyway.

IS A WAY OF TRAVELLING

Happiness is not so much a final destination as a way of journeying through life. There is no need to save up all your happiness for an event or goal somewhere into the distant future, look for happiness today, along the way, as you go. Benjamin Franklin said, "Human felicity is produced not so much by great pieces of good fortune that seldom happen as by little advantages that occur every day."

REACH FOR YOUR DREAMS

Do something each day to bring you a little closer to your dreams.

All the strength you need to achieve anything is within you. Don't wait for a light to appear at the end of the tunnel, stride down there … and light it yourself.

Seeding is believing. If you are seeding positive thoughts and positive habits, then success will eventually blossom. If you're starting to feel itchy and twitchy because change is not happening as speedily as you want, envisage what you want on a delivery truck coming towards you, it's just a bit stuck in traffic but coming towards you right now. The universe's delays are not necessarily the universe's denials.

Ban the words "always" and "never" from your vocabulary. Become aware of using too much "pervasiveness" and "permanence" in your stories.

detox

AFFIRMATIONS TO HELP EMPOWER
YOU TO REACH FOR YOUR DREAMS ...

WISDOM
I dismantle the power struggle
and find my balance

OPTIMISM
I am productive, capable and intelligent

RESPONSIBILITY
I retain my individuality. I actualise my abilities

TENACITY
I choose harmony. I find the balance in my life

HONESTY
I share my feelings. I am able to build trust

WHEN YOU HAVE FAITH IN YOUR ABILITIES AND ACCEPT WHO YOU ARE, YOU WILL UNCOVER YOUR UNIQUE GIFTS ...

Be responsible for yourself.

Work at being a whole human being.

Being able to validate yourself, honestly confront yourself and soothe yourself in difficult moments.

Be a grown-up running your own life.

Honour your goals, challenges and dreams.

Notice the positive. Foster the positive by focusing on what's good.

Make an effort to do little things for people. Small things count.

A small compliment, a loving touch, a little gift, these all feed the wellbeing of others.

Express affection regularly and generously.

Respect everyone's opinions instead of being dogmatic about your own.

Listen and compromise in any given situation.

detox

Don't be afraid of conflict. Be honest even about difficult issues. It is okay if disagreements arise as it's the way you deal with them that makes all the difference.

Make time for fun and humour.

Celebrate love in your idiosyncratic way.

The aim is to manage your life rather than simply let it happen to you. So much unhappiness stems from a lack of control. You shape your life, no-one else.

Change your pattern of thinking now. There is a well-known saying attributed to Abraham Lincoln that "people are usually about as happy as they make up their minds to be."

The Journal of Personality and Social Psychology nominated "autonomy," defined as "the feeling that your life, its activities and habits, are self-chosen and self-endorsed," as important to achieving happiness. Having a strong sense of control of one's life, autonomy, is a more dependable predictor of positive feelings of well-being than any of the objective conditions of life and self-worth.

Women are magnetic beings. Which means that things come to us, always. The only reason we chase anything is when we don't believe in ourselves or are unaware of our power.

Begin each day with saying thank you for three things, no matter how large or small they are. Gratitude leads to contentment, which leads to joy. And joy is a most effective medicine.

Surrender can require just as much strength as resistance. It brings relief and freedom and enlightenment. And often the higher ground, with the grace of it.

Treat your enemy like your best friend. Stun them, soften their heart.

Never forget the power of forgiveness. It can be incredibly releasing — it can flush you clean, uplift you, move you on.

A life lived in fear is a life not fully lived.

detox

     Live with gratitude, entwined with
     your goodness.

     What nourishes the soul — silence, emp-
     tiness, laughter, and nature. A child's
     joy. Rest.

FOR MINDFUL BREATHING ...

Sit for 10 minutes per day. Focus on your breathing,
sit comfortably with your hands on your lap and
close your eyes. Put your hands on your belly to
feel the rise and fall of your breath. Be prepared for
distractions and fidgeting.

FOR MINDFUL LISTENING ...

Gather together household items such as pencils,
paper, coins, or a pot. Place them in a box and close
your eyes, then focus on the individual sounds you
make with them.

FOR MINDFUL SEEING ...

Go to a park. Close your eyes and write in a gratitude
journal descriptions of what you can see.

MINDFUL SMELLING ...

Smell four very different items. For example, peanut butter, a rose, a cinnamon stick and mint. Write down what they remind you of.

MINDFUL TASTING ...

When you eat be aware of the flavours and taste sensations of various foods.

MINDFUL MOVEMENT ...

Turn on the radio and dance.

Levity — humour, lightness, laughter. Nurture these aspects of living for anti-aging effects and good health. The neuroscientist Lee Berk says laughter can make you healthier. It can lower blood pressure, cut stress hormone levels, reduce pain, relax muscles, boost immunity and pump you full of endorphins.

Surround yourself with light. In addition to light-hearted people, surround yourself with lighter images. Take a vacation from the news and get rid of visual negativity.

CHAPTER 8

The mindful brain

MEDITATION

*M*editation combined with yoga promotes physiological as well as mental calming. Since an incredible amount of energy is wasted in maintaining muscle tension when you suffer from stress, you may feel all wound up and thus fatigued. When chronic stress builds up in the muscles, it makes the tendons thicken and shorten due to the over-development of the connective tissue. Stress contributes to the over-activity of the sympathetic nervous system, which results in a build-up of tension in an already taxed nervous system. A quick way to get rid of the build-up of tension and activate the parasympathetic nervous system is to stretch and breathe deeply.

The antithesis of the fight-or-flight response is the relaxation response, which is the body's way of calming itself down. The relaxation response involves activating the parasympathetic nervous system, which promotes a slower heart rate and a slower breathing rate, whereas the fight-or-flight response is activated by the sympathetic nervous system causing the physical and emotional strain to the body.

The brain requires a steady flow of blood, and since the muscles are endowed with a rich blood supply, stretching can facilitate this healthy blood flow required. Stretching, like exercise, promotes an energised capacity to focus combined with a feeling of relaxation. By stretching your muscles, you force or pump the used and de-oxygenated blood back into your heart and lungs for refueling. This results in the replenishment of your brain with re-oxygenated blood. Stretching therefore promotes a refreshed brain, invigorates the muscles and releases built-up tension.

The parts of your brain that make it possible for you to be fully present, with reverence for each moment, have been identified by researchers at the University of Wisconsin, led by Richard Davidson. The cortical networks that involve the front of the cingulate cortex (the part of the brain that is correlated with empathy and self-awareness), the insula (the part of the brain that pays close attention to internal body states), and the somatosensory cortex (the part of the brain that senses our body in space) seem to be activated together.

Using a variety of brain-imaging methods, Davidson and his colleagues examined the brains of Tibetan monks who have practiced meditation for many years. The results show a shift to relatively more activation of the left frontal lobe than of the right frontal lobe. When the monks were asked to generate feelings of compassion, their brain activity indicated that many neural structures were firing in synchrony with one another. The tendency for brain systems to fire synchronously promotes better mental health. Researchers have described the neural circuits of various styles of emotional reactivity and resilience. Mindfulness training can alter these neural functions and promote non-reactivity. Mindfulness meditation promotes an internal attunement that harnesses the social circuits of mirror neurons, which correlate with empathy. There is a sense of empathy for yourself that is cultivated by enhanced self-awareness, and with long-term practice there is an opportunity for greater self-regulation. The top of the temporal lobe pays attention to breathing and then primes the brain to get ready for the next breath. This may contribute to an integration of the sense of self, which leads to harmony between the automatic nervous system and cortical functioning. By enhancing phase synchrony, you are able to feel more present, relaxed and in harmony with yourself and your environment.

When we are in our heads, we are cut off from our hearts, but when we are in our hearts, we can use our heads. These essential life skills allow us to align us to who we really are and what we want and how we show up. When we are able to do this, we become immensely powerful, are able to reach our goals are able to experience peace, even in the midst of chaos.

REMEMBER WHO YOU ARE OR WHO YOU WANT TO BE

Remember who you really are or visualise, imagine, discover or invite that aspect of yourself to be revealed. Look to small children. All the beautiful qualities they possess, their enthusiasm, joy, energy, creativity, imagination, curiosity, playfulness, honesty, and authentic self-expression. None of these qualities go away as we grow up, access simply gets blocked. By remembering who you really are or simply starting to look, you forge the path to your heart.

IDENTIFY YOUR TARGET

onsider what you want to create. Do you want a harmonious relationship, a healthy body, a family, self-esteem, confidence? In order to get what you want, you need to know where you are aiming.

SELF-OBSERVE

ractice self-observation in every moment of every day. Notice what you are doing, saying, and feeling with each step, each word, each thought and each action. Then ask yourself, "Does this serve me? Does this diminish or enhance the obstacles to my goals? If your choices do not serve you, or are not in alignment with who you really are, then it is time to make new choices. Self-observation leads to self-awareness. It allows you the opportunity to make choices. The ability to choose those actions that serve you over those that

detox

don't makes you powerful. In order to get where you want to go, you need to know where you currently are in every given moment.

MAKE THE CHOICE TO LET GO, TO TRANSCEND THE EGO

As you encounter the behaviours, thoughts and words that are not serving you, that are blocking access to your heart, take a breath and make the choice to let them go. Breathe and let go. You will find that ego is always what blocks our access to love, creativity and true power. Ironically, your need for love and your need to be loved are blocking your ability to be loving and to be loved. When encountering obstacles ask yourself, "Is this my need for approval or my need for control that is getting in my way." Once you identify one need, the other or both, breathe and let go. Return your attention to your authentic self.

GET RE-CENTERED, RECALIBRATE, AND GET PRESENT

*E*very time you stop to self-remember, self-observe, let go and get centred you have successfully journeyed from head to heart. The present moment opens the door to your authenticity so you can access your creativity, wisdom, strength and intuition. You are now able to be resourceful. Breathe, reconnect, and replenish. When we are resourceful, a multitude of new options and resources become obvious, available and accessible.

Take aligned action. When your actions (including your thoughts and words) are aligned with who you really are and what you want to create, you become powerful. You are no longer a victim. Your relationships will improve, your joy will return, your energy, creativity, wisdom, compassion, playfulness, curiosity, life purpose and passion will all be accessible once again.

In any given moment in which you feel disconnected, take these simple steps.

121

CHAPTER 9

Self-Acceptance

SELF-ACCEPTANCE

You cannot truly, truly love anyone until you first love yourself. So I want you to pay yourself a compliment, say something sweet to yourself.

You are more than enough, and you are worthy of your best life.

Your dreams are valid. Your goals are valid. The vision for your life is valid. The intention is valid.

You are worthy.

Accept yourself you can't mess up enough
for the creator to fall out of love with
you. He loves you, he loves you.

It's time to let go.

It's time to move on and move forward, accepting
who you are and loving every bit of you.

You are beautiful.

You are fearfully and wonderfully made,
you are gorgeous just the way you are.

125

detox

※※※

Accept you, and love you so you can be a
true extension of love, but first you have
to accept everything about you.

※※※

I want you to close your eyes for just a moment
and imagine yourself standing in front of
yourself and I want you to scan yourself from
the top of your head to the soles of your feet.

※※※

I want you to look in every nook and cranny
and just recognise who you are.

※※※

Paying yourself a compliment looking
at how beautiful you are.

※※※

Looking at how strong you are.

Appreciating that body that has brought you through all of these years of life to right here and right now.

Accept you.

Love you.

Today's the day for that.

Angela Davis, Motivational Coach

About

This is Marianne's 10th book, and she is the author of The Love Trilogy — Love, Love Me, its sequel Things We Love and conclusion Love Always. She is also the author of six additional books and is a media spokesperson, commentator and columnist.

Her work has been featured on the BBC London, NBC Network, Bravo TV, The Huffington Post, Vogue Magazine, Harpers Bazaar, The Guardian, Maxim, The Independent, Cosmopolitan Magazine, Grazia, The Daily Mail, The LA Times and more. Since the launch of her first book in 2008 she has sold her books nationally, and internationally in Europe, the UK, and the USA.

Marianne began her career as a luxury and lifestyle PR executive travelling the globe representing high-end luxury products and high profile celebrity events. She is now known for cresting a new genre of books — self-help inspirational books for girls and women who would not be caught dead reading self help. Her books merge empowering psychology with realistic and tangible verse.

Her eponymous collection of books are available at bookstores and department stores around the world. Get in contact at www.mariannevicelich.com.

Marianne

MARIANNE VICELICH

129